Edward C. Wickham

The Prayer Book

Notes and questions intended to help toward its teaching in the middle

forms of public schools

Edward C. Wickham

The Prayer Book
Notes and questions intended to help toward its teaching in the middle forms of public schools

ISBN/EAN: 9783337012007

Printed in Europe, USA, Canada, Australia, Japan

Cover: Foto ©Paul-Georg Meister /pixelio.de

More available books at **www.hansebooks.com**

THE
PRAYER BOOK

NOTES AND QUESTIONS
INTENDED TO HELP TOWARD ITS TEACHING
IN THE MIDDLE FORMS OF PUBLIC SCHOOLS

BY

E. C. WICKHAM, D.D.

DEAN OF LINCOLN,
FORMERLY MASTER OF WELLINGTON COLLEGE

SECOND EDITION

RIVINGTONS
KING STREET, COVENT GARDEN
LONDON
1897

προσεύξομαι τῷ πνεύματι, προσεύξομαι δὲ καὶ τῷ νοΐ.
1 Cor. xiv. 15.

ἐκβάλλει ἐκ τοῦ θησαυροῦ αὐτοῦ καινὰ καὶ παλαιά.
S. Matt. xiii. 52.

PREFACE TO THE FIRST EDITION

These 'Notes' do not pretend to originality of any kind whatever. They were, most of them, prepared for the strictly practical purpose of helping my colleagues at Wellington College in charge of Middle School Forms to give lectures to their boys on the Prayer Book and to examine them in it, and they were used for several years in this way. They are now printed for wider use, not of my own motion, but in answer to requests which I did not like to refuse.

I have confined the Notes to parts of the Prayer Book with which boys would be most familiar. The Baptismal Service, Catechism, and Confirmation belong to one another, and would receive, no doubt, a different and more complete treatment. The practical purpose in view will explain the omission of many interesting questions, and, so far as possible, of all controversial matter. Brevity was essential.

It is very desirable to give to the Church Services in the eyes of young Churchmen the added interest and dignity which comes from knowing that, in outline and in much of their detail, they are part of the ancient inheritance of Christendom. On the other hand, I should be much more anxious to help boys to feel that our Services, as they stand, are carefully composed, and to follow intelligently their drift and purpose, than to dwell upon the points which difference them from the services of other Communions, or upon the special changes through which they passed between 1549 and 1662.

As before, I have to thank my friend the Rev. Arthur Carr for reading my proof-sheets and for several useful suggestions.

Lincoln, *May* 1895.

CONTENTS

	PAGE
I. Short History of the Book of Common Prayer,	1
II. Notes on the Title-Page, Table of Contents, and Prefaces,	4
III. The Church Year, with Notes	8
(1) on Moveable Feasts,	11
(2) on Some of the Names of Church Seasons,	13
IV. Holy Days, other than the Great Festivals, with a Note on 'Black-Letter Days,'	16
V. Morning and Evening Prayer,	24
VI. The Litany,	39
VII. The Collects, Epistles, and Gospels,	49
VIII. Order of the Administration of the Lord's Supper or Holy Communion,	54

I.

SHORT HISTORY

OF THE BOOK OF COMMON PRAYER

It dates, in a sense, from the Reformation, but this does not mean that the prayers were, most of them, composed then. What was done was to rearrange, shorten, and translate into English, the Service Books already in use in the English Church.

These, which were in Latin, were chiefly:

1. The *Breviary* ('Breviarium,' so called as an abbreviation of a still longer collection of services) or Daily Offices. This was very long, and was used chiefly by the clergy or in monasteries.
2. The *Missal* ('Missale' from *missa* the Mass, the Latin name for the service of Holy Communion. *See* p. 56).

The purposes with which our Prayer Book was put together are:

1. While retaining as much as possible of the ancient services, *to omit what was thought inconsistent with truth and primitive doctrine,*

prayers addressed to saints, legends or traditions not found in Holy Scripture, ceremonies which were held superfluous or which had led to abuse.

2. To fit the services for the intelligent and profitable *use of the general congregation*. It is this purpose which gives its special force to the title chosen, 'Book of Common Prayer.' (This title, as seems from the title-page, belongs especially to the Daily Services, since it is distinguished from the 'Administration of the Sacraments,' etc. *Cp.* the phrase 'common supplications' in the 'Prayer of St. Chrysostom.') With this view the services were (1) translated into English; (2) shortened and simplified, especial care being taken that the arrangements for the use of the Psalms and the reading of the Bible should be complete and continuous. (*See* the Prefaces to the Prayer Book.)

There have been five editions of the Prayer Book, some alterations being made in each new edition.

1. The first Prayer Book of King Edward vi., 1549, prepared by a Commission with Archbishop Cranmer at its head.
2. The second Prayer Book of King Edward vi., 1552.
This was a revision of the first, made in consequence of complaints that the changes from Roman use had not been great enough. The Book was ordered to be brought into use

on All Saints' Day, 1552, but the king died
in July 1553, before its use had become
general, and was succeeded by Queen Mary
who restored the Roman services. Many,
however, of the alterations made in it were
retained in the next revision under Queen
Elizabeth. Amongst these was the placing of
the Sentences, Exhortation, Confession, and
Absolution at the beginning of Morning and
Evening Prayer, these services having in the
first book of Edward VI. begun with the Lord's
Prayer.

3. Queen Elizabeth's, 1559.

The Prayer Book of 1552 was the basis of this
edition, but a few changes were made in order
to meet the wishes of those who preferred the
Book of 1549. For an instance, *see* p. 63.

4. King James I.'s, 1604.

Issued after the Conference between the Bishops
and Puritan Divines, called the 'Hampton Court
Conference.'

5. King Charles II.'s, 1662.

The Restoration Prayer Book, issued after the
'Savoy Conference.' No alterations have been
made in it since that date, except in respect
of the Table of Lessons which was changed in
1871 and of the Special National Services.
See p. 7

II
NOTES
ON THE TITLE-PAGE,
TABLE OF CONTENTS, AND PREFACES

I. THE TITLE-PAGE.

Notice (1) the distinction between 'The Church' 'and the Church of England.' 'The Sacraments and other Rites and Ceremonies' are spoken of as belonging to 'the Church,' *i.e.* the Church Catholic; the *'use'* as belonging to the Church of England.

(2) the meaning of this word *'use.'* Forms of prayer and observance to be used in the celebration of the Lord's Supper and on other occasions grew up gradually. They differed in different places, resting (1) on the authority of the bishop in each diocese; (2) on custom. The Latin word for such forms was *usus*. The 'use' generally prevalent in England at the time of the Reformation was the 'use of Sarum,' *i.e.* of the diocese of Salisbury, which had been adopted in other dioceses. When the Prayer Book was drawn up, one 'use' was adopted for the whole of the National Church.

II. THE CONTENTS OF THE BOOK AND THEIR ORDER.

1. The PREFACES, TABLE OF LESSONS, ETC.
   Lessons (Fr. *leçons*, Lat. *lectiones*) *readings.*
2. The order of DAILY PRAYERS, Morning and Evening.
   The older and alternative names are given in the Table of Lessons:
   Mattins (or Matins. Fr. *matins*, Lat. *matutinae* [preces]).
   Evensong, literal translation of the old name Vespers (Fr. *vêpres*, Lat. *vespertinae* [preces]; evening' prayers) 'song,' because the service in old days was always 'sung' or 'chanted' (Fr. *chanté*, Lat. *cantus*).

   To this is added as an appendix:
   1. The 'Athanasian' Creed, which is to be substituted on certain mornings for the 'Apostles' Creed.
   2. The Litany to be used 'after Morning Prayer' on certain days.
   3. Prayers and thanksgivings to be added on occasions to the Daily Prayers.
3. The COLLECTS, EPISTLES, AND GOSPELS, which mark the seasons of the Church's *year.*
   These belong properly to the Communion Service, but enter also, through the Collect, into the Daily Service, and the Collect, Epistle, and Gospel for a Sunday are ordered to be used through the *week.*

4. The SACRAMENTAL Services, viz.—

    1. The Order of Holy Communion.
    2. The Order of Holy Baptism, in three forms:
        (1) for Infants—when baptized in Church.
        (2) for Infants—when baptized privately.
        (3) for Adults.

To these are appended, as closely related to both Sacraments,

    (1) The *Catechism*. Note its second title, and its position between the Baptismal and Confirmation Services.
    (2) The order of *Confirmation*, in which the young Christian makes his own the promises of Baptism and is admitted by the Church to the reception of the other Sacrament.

5. The OCCASIONAL Services
    (1) which have to do with the great events of human life: marriage—sickness—death—birth.
    (2) the Special Lenten Service, the 'Commination.'

6. The PSALTER, divided for daily use through the *month*.

7. Some prayers *to be used at sea* [interesting as showing how large a part the Navy had in the nation's life].

8. The ORDINAL, or making of Deacons, Priests, Bishops.

9. Special *National* Service on the *Accession of the Sovereign*.

N.B.—There used to be others, still to be seen in older Prayer Books, for January 30, May 29, November 5, anniversaries of great events in the national history.

III. THE PREFACES

The first Preface belongs to the last revision of the Book, viz., in 1662, and describes the purpose of that revision. It is said to have been written by Bishop Sanderson of Lincoln.

The second ('concerning the Service of the Church') and the third ('of Ceremonies, why some be abolished, and some retained') belong to the Prayer Book of 1549, and are said to be due to Cranmer. The former of these was the original Preface, and describes the chief purposes with which the Book was drawn up. The latter stood in the Book of 1549 as a note at the end, but in the first revision (1552) was removed to the beginning as a second Preface.

III

THE CHURCH YEAR

THE *idea* of it is to arrange the Readings and Services so that in each year (1) the chief events of the Gospel Story, (2) the chief subjects of the teaching of our Lord and His Apostles, should be brought before our minds in an orderly way.

This is chiefly done through the Collects, Epistles, and Gospels, though on the greater days the same character is impressed on special Psalms, Lessons, and other parts of the Service.

From *Advent to Whitsunday* the *events* are gone through chronologically, from the Incarnation to the Descent of the Holy Spirit.

On *Trinity Sunday* we sum up what we have learnt in the course of these events about God's Nature—one God, yet in Three Persons—the Father, the Son, and the Holy Spirit.

The *Sundays that follow* are given generally to the moral and religious *teaching* of Christ and His Apostles.

The *Events* divide themselves into two parts grouped round (1) Christmas (2) Easter.

1. CHRISTMAS ('the Nativity of our Lord, or the Birthday of Christ, commonly called Christmas Day'). For meaning of the word, *see* p. 13.
  preceded by *Advent*—a time of preparation for it, which consists in thinking what Christ's '*Coming*' means—His first coming and His second.
  followed by (1) the *Circumcision* on the 8th day after Christmas (St. Luke ii. 21, Gen. xvii. 12).
   - (2) The *Epiphany*—or 'manifestation' of the Infant Saviour to the wise men from the East.
   - The Sundays which follow take up generally the subject of the manifestation of Christ's glory and power (1) in the Divine Boyhood, (2) during His ministry, in the miracles of various kinds, (3) in His return (6th Sunday) at the end of the world.

2. EASTER—*preceded* by Lent and the Week of the Passion:
  followed by the 'great forty days' (Acts i. 3), the Ascension, and Whitsuntide.
   - (1) *Lent* itself is introduced by three Sundays called by Latin names: Septuagesima, Sexagesima, Quinquagesima (for the names, *see* p. 14), as it is itself called in Latin 'Quadragesima.'
   - It begins on Ash Wednesday, and lasts (*in round numbers*) forty days.

As the Epiphany season had to do with the manifestation in Christ's Life of glory and power, so Lent turns our thoughts to His suffering and the cause of it, viz. human *sin*. The 'forty days' are in special commemoration of His forty days (St. Matt. iv. 2) of fasting and temptation in the wilderness. This is taken as the beginning of His *suffering* life, as the Passion is the end of it.

(2) Then follows the *Week of the Passion*,[1] in which we are meant to follow day by day the events of the week as detailed in all the four Evangelists from the triumphal entry into Jerusalem on the first day (Palm Sunday) to the Last Supper, the Betrayal and Agony, on Thursday evening; the Crucifixion on Good Friday; the Resting in the Tomb on Saturday (the Jewish 'Sabbath'—Easter Even).

(3) *Easter Day*—the day of the Resurrection.

(4) *Ascension Day*—(also called in the Prayer Book 'Holy Thursday') exactly forty days after Easter.

---

[1] *N.B.*—Although the terms are not used in the Prayer Book, it is common to speak of the week before Easter as Passion Week, or, more frequently still, Holy Week. 'Passion Sunday,' on the other hand, is an ancient name given to the Fifth Sunday in Lent, on which the Epistle and Gospel begin for the first time definitely to refer to our Lord's Rejection and Sufferings, the Sunday before Easter being called Palm Sunday, from the circumstances of the entry into Jerusalem.

This, like the other greater Festivals, has some days of preparation, called (*see* the list of 'days of fasting') 'Rogation days.' ('Rogationes,' an old name meaning the same as 'Litanies.' *See* p. 39.)

(5) *Whitsunday*—'the Day of Pentecost' (Acts ii. 1), when the Holy Spirit descended on the Infant Church, *fifty days* after Easter.

NOTES

I. ON MOVEABLE FEASTS

It will be noticed that, of the two series of Festivals described, the first, viz. Christmas, and those dependent on it, are on *fixed days* (with the exception that Advent Sunday, being the Fourth *Sunday* before Christmas Day, will vary as to the day of the *month* within six days, according to the day of the *week* on which Christmas Day falls). The second, viz. Easter, and those dependent on it, *vary from year to year*. The reason is to be found in the history of their observance.

Christmas, the Circumcision, and the Epiphany, like most other holidays of the Christian Calendar, were in origin *independent of Jewish tradition*. They were fixed at first differently by different churches, but eventually December 25 was generally accepted as the determining day.

Easter was, no doubt, observed from the first as an anniversary, and, as the first Christians were Jews, it would naturally be fixed in accordance with the

Jewish Calendar; and the point which would be most remembered would be that the Crucifixion and Resurrection happened *during the Passover* (St. Matt. xxvi. 2). This was fixed more definitely by the fact that the Church, following St. Paul (1 Cor. v. 7), saw in the Paschal deliverance of Israel from Egypt, with the circumstances that accompanied it, a type of the deliverance of mankind from sin and death by our Lord's Death and Resurrection. (*See* the Psalms and lessons for Easter Day.)

In the same way the event of Whitsunday, which we know to have happened on the Jewish Pentecost (Acts ii. 1) or 'Feast of Weeks' fifty days after the Passover (Lev. xxiii. 16), was commemorated at the time of that Festival.

Now, the Jewish Calendar was *lunar*; that is, a 'month' meant, not, as with us, the twelfth part of a solar year of 365 days 6 hours, but a *perfect lunar month, i.e.* the exact time between new moon and new moon—the first day of every month being the day of a new moon. The Passover was kept on 'the fourteenth day of the first month'[1] (Exod. xii. 18), *i.e.* at a *full moon somewhere near the spring equinox*, but varying necessarily in exact date from year to year.

Our rule is *based upon this*, viz., that EASTER SUNDAY IS THE SUNDAY AFTER THE FULL MOON WHICH HAPPENS ON OR NEXT AFTER MARCH 21. This may be as early as March 22 or as late as April 25.

[In keeping Easter we remember always the other fixed point, viz., that our Lord rose 'on

[1] Called *Abib* in Exod. xxiii. 15, etc., *Nisan* in Neh. ii. 1, etc.

the *first day of the week*' (St. Matt. xxviii. 1), whereas the Passover was kept on the full moon, whatever day of the week it happened to be. For this reason (not to mention other changes of detail which have happened both to the Jewish Calendar and to our own), our Easter does not generally coincide actually with the present Jewish observance of the Passover, though by its variations it preserves the memory of its original connection with the Passover.]

As Lent is forty days before Easter, and the Ascension forty days after it, Septuagesima and the Sundays that follow it until Trinity Sunday will vary in date as Easter varies. This causes also the number of Sundays after the Epiphany and those between Trinity and Advent to vary.

II. ON SOME OF THE NAMES OF CHURCH SEASONS

Christmas—'mas' from 'mass,' English form of the Latin *missa*, the Roman name [1] for the celebration of the Lord's Supper; and thence used for any Church festival: so also 'Michaelmas'; and in older writings Hallowmas = All Saints' Day; Lammas for Aug. 1 (from loaf), an old harvest festival, etc.

Other names of it: In the Prayer Book—'the Nativity or Birthday of Christ.' So the Fr. *Noël*, a shortened form of Lat. *natalis*. Ger. *Weihnacht*—Holy night.

[1] For explanation of the word, see p. 56.

Septuagesima, Sexagesima, Quinquagesima—These correspond to the name Quadragesima or 'fortieth,' which is given to Lent. The origin of this is not quite certain; but, in any case, it was taken eventually to refer to its length as of (roughly) forty days before Easter. Then Lent being called Quadragesima, the week immediately before it was called Quinquagesima, and the Sunday in it Dominica in Quinquagesima; and so with the other two.

Lent—An Anglo-Saxon word *Lencten*, which only meant 'Spring.' The Latin Quadragesima becomes in Italian Quaresima, and in French Carême.

Easter—Again an Anglo-Saxon name—so in Ger. *Ostern*—derived from a Teutonic goddess (*cp.* our names of the week, Tuesday, Thursday, Friday), Eastre or Eostre, whose festival came in April.

The Latin name is *Pascha* (the Passover), whence Fr. *Pâques*. Pascha ($\Pi\acute{\alpha}\sigma\chi\alpha$) was a putting into a Greek form of the Heb. *Pesach*, which means 'to leap over.' The word 'Passover' in our Bible is an attempt to *translate* the Hebrew word.

Whitsunday — Whitsuntide. The derivation is a matter of controversy. The one best supported (see Skeat's *Etymological Dictionary*), as well as the most picturesque, is that from 'White-Sunday,' *i.e.* the day on which newly baptized persons appeared in their white Baptismal Dress. It is thus exactly parallel to the Lat. *Dominica in Albis*, the name given for the same reason to the Sunday after Easter. Easter and Whitsunday were the great times for Baptism, and it is said that in our colder climate Whitsuntide was preferred. 'Whitsuntide,' 'Whitsun week,' are in this case the abbreviations for 'Whitsunday-tide, etc. *N.B.*—That though we often talk of 'Whit-Monday,' the only title known to the Prayer Book is the 'Monday in Whitsun week.'

Other suggestions are:

(1) Some corruption of the Ger. *Pfingst*—itself a corruption of Pentecost.
(2) Some connection with 'wit,' 'wis-dom'—the time when the Spirit of Wisdom came to men.

IV

HOLY DAYS,

OTHER THAN THE GREAT FESTIVALS

HOLY days are of two kinds:

1. Joyous — called *Feasts* or Festivals, Fr. *fêtes* — from Latin *dies festi*, holidays (*festus*, by derivation, meant 'bright,' 'cheerful'), opp. *dies profesti*, 'working days.'
2. Mournful — called *Fasts* — times of strictness, serious thought, self-denial: the word is the same as the adj. 'fast' = tight, fixed—used in the wider sense of *strict*. It was then employed as the translation (as it is in German) of the Latin *jejunium* (Fr. *jeûne*), *i.e.* time of abstinence from food, or from food of a certain kind.

I. FEASTS.

These are the commemorations of

1. Further incidents of the Incarnation.
   (1) The *Annunciation* to the Blessed Virgin Mary of Christ's coming Birth.
   St. Luke i. 26.

(2) The *Purification* (*i.e.* as we should say, the 'churching') of the Blessed Virgin, forty days after His Birth, and the Presentation at the same time of the Infant Saviour in the Temple. St. Luke ii. 22-24.

2. The Apostles, and others closely connected with our Lord's life on earth, and the first starting of the Church; the Forerunner, St. John the Baptist; the Holy Innocents; the Evangelists, St. Mark and St. Luke (St. Matthew and St. John being also Apostles); the first Martyr, St. Stephen; St. Paul, the Apostle of the Gentiles, and his brother Apostle Barnabas.[1]

3. All Saints—'the great multitude that no man can number.' Rev. vii. 9.

4. The ministry of Holy Angels (Michaelmas).

Notice (1) that our Church has limited this public commemoration in her services to those persons of whom she can find materials for her reading in Holy Scripture itself. In the festival of All Saints she allows the principle that there are others not unworthy to be ranked as Saints, but the list is left to each to fill for himself.

---

[1] St. James (the Less) and St. Jude, the Lord's 'brethren,' are fitly included as writers of Epistles in the Canon; but they were, no doubt, thought to be also of the number of the Twelve, being identified with 'James the son of Alphæus, and Thaddæus' (St. Matt. x. 3), an identification probably wrong. *See* Bishop Lightfoot's excursus on 'The Brethren of the Lord' in his *Galatians*.

(2) that in the arrangement of the Holy Days through the year we can see sometimes a special purpose, *e.g.* the Purification is forty days after the Nativity (Lev. xii. 3, 4); St. John the Baptist, on June 24, because John was born six months before our Blessed Lord. St. Andrew, one of the two first called of the Apostles (St. John i. 40), has the first Saint's Day in the year. All Saints' Day is the last.

Some appropriateness may also be seen in the Church seasons to which certain festivals are assigned.

The two, for instance, which fall generally in the Epiphany season, are those of the Conversion of St. Paul (the great preacher to the Gentile world) and the Presentation of Christ in the Temple. The three which follow Christmas Day seem chosen to illustrate the witness borne to the new-born Saviour by different types of life and character.

II. FASTS

These are

1. The time of Lent—especially the First Day of Lent, Ash-Wednesday.
2. All Fridays, in memory of Good Friday, and of human sin, which was the cause of the event which happened on it.
3. The *Eves* or *Vigils* before most Feasts, *see* the list in the Calendar.

The day before any Feast is called an *Eve* (Ger. *abend*), *i.e.* properly, 'the evening before.' When the Eve was intended to be kept as a

Fast Day it was called a 'Vigil,' Lat. *vigilia*, a time of watching. The French distinguish the two senses by two different forms of the same word derived from *vigilia*, 'veille' in the sense merely of the day preceding a Feast, and then, as our 'eve,' metaphorically, 'la veille de la bataille'—'vigile' in a sense of a time of watching and self-denial before a Feast.

4. The Rogation Days—the three days before the Ascension Day. [For the original observance of these see p. 40. It became general, the particular objects of the prayers offered being a blessing on the coming harvest, freedom from pestilence and from war. The custom still observed in some places of 'beating the bounds' on the day before Ascension Day, is a relic of the old 'Rogations' or Litanies sung in procession, a Christian 'ambarvalia' (VIRG. *Ecl.* 5. 75, *Georg.* 1. 338-350).]

5. The Ember Days — (the name from A.S. *ymbren*—a course or circuit—days that come round at fixed seasons. It has no etymological connection with the German name for them, *quatember*, which is a corruption of *quatuor tempora*). They are the Wednesday, Friday, and Saturday after
   First Sunday in Lent, Whit Sunday,
   September 14, December 13,
and precede the times at which Ordination is ordinarily administered, and are in imitation of Apostolic practice (Acts xiii. 8).

NOTE ON BLACK-LETTER DAYS

Although commemoration in the Church services was limited in the reformed Prayer Book, as has been explained, a further selection from the days previously observed was retained in the Calendar, the names being printed in *black* instead of *red*. Some of these seem to have owed their retention to practical reasons, as that they were recognised dates for law business, fairs, and other local and particular arrangements; others, no doubt, owed it to historical and other interest.

They include:

1. Further commemorations of our Lord and of New Testament saints. Such are the Transfiguration (Aug. 6); three further Festivals of the Blessed Virgin (July 2, Sept. 8, Dec. 8), and one (July 26) of her mother, St. Anne, known to very early tradition, though not named in the New Testament; the Beheading of John the Baptist (Aug. 29); St. Mary Magdalene (July 22); St. John the Evangelist *ante portam Latinam* (May 6), commemorating the story of St. John's deliverance when cast, by Domitian's orders, into a caldron of boiling oil before the *Porta Latina* at Rome. Two days, May 13, 'Invention of the Cross,' and Sept. 14, 'Holy Cross Day,' are named from incidents in the legend of the recovery of the true Cross by Helena, the mother of Constantine.

2. Some of the martyrs in the early persecutions, as St. Lawrence, St. Valentine, St. Agnes, St. Cæcilia, St. Catharine, etc.
3. Some of the most famous of the fathers of the Church, as St. Clement of Rome, St. Jerome, St. Ambrose, St. Augustine (Bishop of Hippo).
4. Some of the saints specially connected with the history of the Church in our islands and in France. Such are:—

> St. George (April 23), an Eastern saint and martyr, said to have been taken as the patron saint of England during the Crusades, there being a story of his having appeared with a banner marked with a red cross and led an army against the Saracens.
> Alban (June 17), the first British martyr.
> David, Archbishop of Menevia (March 1), the Welsh saint.
> Gregory the Great (March 12), the Pope who sent Augustine to convert the English.
> Augustine, first Archbishop of Canterbury (May 26), the Apostle of England.
> Etheldreda (Oct. 17), founder of the Abbey of Ely.
> Chad (March 2), founder of Lichfield Cathedral.
> The Venerable Bede (May 27), the historian of the early English Church. Died A.D. 735.

Boniface, Bishop of Mentz (June 5), an Englishman, the Apostle of Germany.

Swithin (July 15), founder of Winchester Cathedral.

Three sainted Anglo-Saxon Kings: Edmund, king of East Anglia (Nov. 20); Edward, king of West Saxons (March 18); K. Edward the Confessor (Oct. 13).

Dunstan (May 19), the champion of monasticism.

Hugh (Nov. 17), the great Bishop of Lincoln, and rebuilder of its Cathedral.

To these may be added of French saints:

St. Denys (Dionysius) (Oct. 9), patron saint of France, often wrongly identified with Dionysius the Areopagite (Acts xvii. 34).

Hilary of Poitiers (Jan. 13) — we still speak of the Spring Law Term as Hilary Term.

St. Martin of Tours (Nov. 11).

Remigius of Rheims (Oct. 6), who converted Clovis.

Crispin (said, with his brother Crispian, or Crispinian, to have worked as a shoemaker, and therefore the patron saint of shoemakers), October 25, the day of Agincourt; Shakspeare, *Henry V.*, Act IV., Scene iii., 'Crispin Crispian shall ne'er go by,' etc.

Giles, Abbot and Confessor (Sept. 1), the patron of cripples.

5. Lammas (Aug. 1) has been explained on p. 13.

'*O Sapientia*' (Dec. 16) is not a holy day, but the first words of the first of a series of antiphons which were sung with the Magnificat on each day between Dec. 16 and Christmas Eve.

V

MORNING AND EVENING PRAYER

NOTICE the sentence at the beginning, 'At the beginning of Prayer the Minister shall, etc.' What are such directions called?

> [*Rubrica*—a classical Latin term for a law—properly the first words of the law written as a heading in red, cp. 'rubras majorum leges,' *Juv. S.* 14, 192. *Rubrica* is properly 'red earth,' 'red ochre.']

1. The Sentences, Exhortation, Confession, Absolution form together the *introduction* to the Service, and were added at the first revision of the Prayer Book in 1552.

The *Sentences* are texts, encouraging us to repentance and confession.

Some need a word of explanation, *e.g.*—

> 'Rend your heart'—the figure.
>
> 'Correct me, but with judgement,' *i.e.* with measure. It is interpreted by 'not in thine anger.'
>
> 'Enter not into judgement'—a different use of judgement.' 'Do not bring me to trial at Thy tribunal.' 'Justified,' acquitted—pronounced 'not guilty.'

The *Exhortation.*

> Notice that it sets out the *essential parts of public worship*:

1. Thanksgiving.
2. Praise.
3. Hearing of God's Word.
4. Prayer for what is needed both for body and soul.
5. That which is right at all times, but especially suitable and needful as completing, and making us fit for, these others—viz. *Confession* of sin.

The *Confession.*

> 'A general confession'—*i.e.* a confession in which all are to join. It is understood, of course, that those who use it think of their own particular failings, what they have themselves 'done' and 'left undone.' They acknowledge them in these general terms to God and to their brethren (St. James v. 16), and receive the assurance of forgiveness together.
>
> 'We have erred and strayed from thy ways like lost sheep.' Isa. liii. 6; Ps. cxix. 176.
>
> 'devices'—plans—fancies.
>
> 'we have left undone, etc.' Rom. vii. 19.
>
> 'health,' *i.e.* moral health—*salus.*
>
> 'godly, righteous, and sober.' Tit. ii. 12.
>> These three words relate to our conduct towards God, our neighbour, and ourselves.

'*Amen*,' a Hebrew adverb of affirmation—'assuredly,' 'so be it'—used in the Synagogue at the end of prayers: adopted from thence into the Christian service, *see* 1 Cor. xiv. 16.

In our Prayer Book a distinction is observed according as it is printed in *italics*—when it is a response, the people thereby assenting to, and joining in, what has been said by the Minister—or in *Roman* type. In the latter case it is part of the Prayer, and is said by the same person or persons as say the Prayer, whether this be Minister and people together, *as here*, and in the Lord's Prayer generally; or the Minister alone, as in the Lord's Prayer at the beginning of the Communion Service.

The '*Absolution* or Remission of sins.'

Absolution—Latin *absolutio*, from *absolvo*—the regular Latin word for declaring a person not guilty, acquitting, whether formally in a law court or in common life. [Notice in the rubric the word 'pronounce' (*pronunciare*) of formal and authoritative declaration, as of a judge or of an ambassador, so in the Marriage Service, 'I pronounce that they be man and wife.']

Remission of sins—the common phrase in the New Testament, as in St. Luke xxiv. 47, for God's forgiveness of sin.

The prayer consists of three parts:
1. A *statement of the authority* for 'pronouncing' absolution and the *condition* on which it is effectual ('being penitent').
   [*cp.* especially St Luke xxiv. 47: 'That repentance and remission of sins should be preached in His name among all nations.' Also St. John xx. 23, which is referred to in the ordination of Priests.]
2. The *declaration of God's absolution* of those who repent.
3. An exhortation to those present to *pray for grace* to fit them for this absolution.

The *Lord's Prayer.*

'The Lord's,' because given by our Lord Jesus Christ. Given *twice* as the model of prayer: for the mixed multitude (St. Matt. vi. 9), and for the Apostles (St. Luke xi. 2).

Its use in Church Services.

Notice (1) its frequency—no Service without it.

(2) its place—always either at the actual beginning of the Service, or when prayer is beginning, or beginning again, after praise or reading. In Morning Prayer we have it twice—here, *i.e.* at the beginning of the Service proper, after the introduction, and when prayer begins again after the Psalms, Lessons, and Creed. So in the Communion Service at the beginning, and before the prayers after the Communion itself.

It is meant to set the tone of the prayers that follow.

(3) the rubric which orders that it is to be repeated by the people with the minister here and wherever it is used in Divine Service. There is an exception to this usage at the beginning of the Communion Service where it is said by the Priest alone.

(4) the Doxology (what does this word mean ?).

Notice (1) that it does not properly belong to the Lord's Prayer itself. It is found in the A.V. in St. Matthew—not in St. Luke—but in the R.V. it is not in either. It is not found in the earliest MSS. of the New Testament. It was used in Church Services in early times, and from this became attached to the Prayer in copies of the Gospel also.

(2) that it is not generally used in the Prayer Book —only *twice*, where the Lord's Prayer precedes a Service of praise—here before the Psalms, and in the Communion Service before the Prayer of Thanksgiving and the Hymn—not the second time that it is used in Daily Prayer, nor the first time in the Communion Service.

The '*Versicles*'—*versiculi*, 'short lines,' 'half verses.'

Notice (1) that they come from the Psalms.

'O Lord, open thou our lips.' 'And our mouth shall shew forth Thy praise,' from Ps. li. 15.

'O Lord, make speed to save us.' 'O Lord, make haste to help us,' from Ps. lxx. 1.

(2) that they do not quite literally follow our version of the Psalms is due to the fact that they are one of the oldest parts of the service, and so are translated from the old Latin services, not directly from the Psalms.

'*Glory be, etc.*'—We begin here the *Service of Praise*—and we begin it with this distinctively Christian ascription of Glory to God. It is of great antiquity, but the origin is not known. It stands in the same place in the ancient services both of the Eastern and Western Churches.

'*Praise ye the Lord.*'—A translation of the Hebrew ascription 'Hallelujah.'

The *Venite*.

The first word in Latin is given, as in the case of the *Te Deum laudamus*, etc. The purpose no doubt in the first instance was to make the people see that they were the Psalms and Hymns to which they had been accustomed.

The 95th Psalm—called from verses 1, 2, 6, 8, *Psalmus invitatorius*. It has been used from the earliest times at the beginning of the Daily Service.

It may be noticed that (like the Exhortation) it touches the different parts of Divine Service.

    Praise and thanksgiving, vv. 1-5.

    Prayer, vv. 6, 7.

    Hearing of God's Word, v. 8.

    Confession of sinfulness is suggested in the last verses.

'in the provocation,' 'day of temptation'—these are translations of the Hebrew names 'Meribah' and 'Massah,' which were given to the place where the people thirsted for water and murmured against Moses (Exod. xvii. 7; Deut. xxxiii. 8). Notice that this part of the Psalm is commented on, in a Christian sense, in Heb. iii. 7-19.

The *Psalms*.

1. What are the Psalms? The inspired hymn-book of the Jewish Church—'The Psalms of David'—not because they are all by him,—for many bear on their face that they were composed in or after the Captivity (*e.g.* cxxvi., cxxxvii.),—but because he composed some, and because he first organised the musical part of the public service of God (1 Chron. xxv. 1-7).

They were used in the Temple service, and also in private devotion. They were often on our Lord's lips. At the Last Supper, when it is said that they 'sung a hymn,' this was probably what the Jews called the 'Hallel' or 'Praise,' which was usually sung at the Passover meal, viz. Psalms cxiii.-cxviii. Two of our Lord's sayings on the Cross were quotations from the Psalms. Ps. xxii. 1; xxxi. 5; St. Matt. xxvii. 46; St. Luke xxiii. 46.

The Psalms, then, are the inspired expression of the penitence, the aspirations, the devotion, the thanksgiving, the patriotism, of saints and prophets 'of old time.' But we have been taught more perfectly than they the mind of God on some points. When we use them, therefore, in the Christian service as the expression of our devotion, we are meant to use them *in a Christian sense*. This is implied by our adding to each Psalm the Christian doxology.

2. The Psalms have always been used in Christian services; but the arrangement of them has been very various. Our Prayer Book arranges them so that they are gone through in a month.
3. Read the 'Order how the Psalter is appointed to be read,' with the note at the end of it, in the Preface to the Prayer Book. This explains why the Prayer Book Psalms do not correspond exactly to the Psalms as they stand in our Bibles. There have been several editions of the English Bible as there have of the Prayer Book. The first published with authority was that known as Cranmer's Bible in 1540. The Psalms in the Prayer Book are taken from that version. In 1662 other parts of Scripture, which appear in the services, were assimilated to the 'Authorised Version,' *i.e.* that which we still use, and which was published in 1611 under James I.; but the old version was retained in the Psalms from consideration for choirs, and as the more musical, and also because it had become familiar and endeared to many in devotional use.

The older version had been made from the Vulgate (or Latin Bible) as that had been, in the Psalms, from the Septuagint (or Greek Bible), with little or no reference to the Hebrew text. One curious instance of this may be seen in Ps. xiv., where the Prayer Book version has eleven verses, the Bible version only seven—the Prayer Book following the Latin and Greek in the insertion of vv. 4-7. This was apparently due, in the first instance, to an error in some MS. of the Septuagint, owing to some one remembering the quotation of Ps. xiv. in Rom. iii. 10-12, and thinking that the following verses, 13-18, were a continuation of the same quotation, whereas they are quotations from several Psalms put together, St. Paul's purpose being to show that the depravity of human nature was witnessed to not in one, but in many places in the Old Testament Scriptures.

4. Another trace of the Vulgate is in the Latin headings of the Psalms, 'Venite exultemus,' 'Beatus vir,' etc., which are the first words of the Psalms in the Latin version, the Psalms having been generally known by their first words instead of a number, just as the Lord's Prayer was called 'Pater noster,' and the Creed 'Credo.'

The *Lessons*. (Fr. *leçons*, Lat. *lectiones*, 'readings' from Holy Scripture.)

The *Rubric*. 'Then shall be read, etc.'

Notice (1) the emphasis laid on the point that they are to be read so that they can be *heard* by every one. This was most important when Bibles were scarce and when the public reading of the Bible was a novelty, but it still is in place.

(2) that the phrase 'he that readeth' (substituted in 1662 for 'the Minister that readeth') was deliberately intended to allow *laymen* to read the lessons.

The *reading of Scripture as part of Divine Service* is another feature inherited from the Jewish Church. In the service of the Synagogue there were two 'Lessons': one from the 'Law' (Pentateuch), one from the Prophets. *See* St. Luke iv. 16, 17; Acts xiii. 15; xv. 21.

The *Table of Lessons* (often called 'Lectionary'). There have been two in our Church since the Reformation:
(1) framed in 1549, and continued, with slight modifications, in the later editions of the Prayer Book.
(2) framed in 1871 (the 'new Lectionary').
Both these follow, in many points, the usage of ancient times as to the parts of Scripture read at special times of the year, *e.g.* Isaiah in Advent, Genesis on Septuagesima and following Sundays, etc.

The *Canticles*[1] (*cantica*, 'songs'). Hymns or Psalms used after the Lessons.
These, with exception of the Te Deum and the Benedicite, are all from Holy Scripture, both at Morning and at Evening Prayer.

The *Te Deum*. An ancient Christian Hymn. The tradition is that it was composed by St. Ambrose (Bp. of Milan) and St. Augustine (Bp. of Hippo, in Africa), at the Baptism of the latter, in 387 A.D., each Saint contributing a verse alternately. Some sentences of it are found much earlier than this, and it is probable that the hymn grew up gradually.

---

[1] This name is given in the Prayer Book only to the *Benedicite*, but it is very commonly extended to the other Hymns and Psalms used at this place in the Service, and indeed to the *Venite* also.

Its contents combine

(1) a *hymn* of praise to God from all creation;
(2) a *creed* or confession of faith in the Holy Trinity, the Incarnation, Resurrection, Ascension, Eternal Judgement, Redemption;
(3) a *prayer* for blessings and graces.

The *Benedicite*. This comes from the Apocrypha, *i.e.* those Books, or parts of Books which formed part of the sacred Jewish literature, but which were not put by the Jews into the 'Canon,' or list, of Holy Scripture. It is to be found in any Bible which contains the Apocrypha, and is called there '*the Song of the Three Children.*' It was an addition to the Book of Daniel, being inserted in the Septuagint (or Greek translation of the Old Testament) between verses 23 and 24 of Dan. iii. It purports to be the song sung by Shadrach, Meshach, and Abednego while in the fiery furnace of Nebuchadnezzar. Their proper Hebrew names (*see* Dan. i. 7) were Hananiah (in Greek Ananias), Mishael, and Azariah, the names that appear in this song.

It is an appeal to all nature to join the Church in ascription of praise to God.

The *Benedictus*, the song of Zacharias, St. Luke i. 68. It is headed, in an earlier edition of the Prayer Book, 'a Thanksgiving for the fulfilment of God's promises,' and this is its purpose as used after the Lesson from the New Testament.

The *Jubilate*. Psalm c. a triumphal hymn, 'All people that on earth do dwell,' an alternative to the Benedictus, especially on days when that has been read in the Lesson.

The Evening Canticles.

The *Magnificat* (the name, as with Psalms, from the first word in the Vulgate), St. Luke i. 46. The hymn of the Blessed Virgin after Elizabeth's salutation of her as 'the mother of my Lord.'

Note that the Lesson from the New Testament is preceded and followed both in Morning and Evening Prayer by a Christian hymn of praise to God for the Incarnation of our Lord. The hymns in the Morning are more jubilant, those in the Evening more of peaceful satisfaction.

As an alternative, Psalm xcvi., *Cantate Domino*.

The *Nunc Dimittis* or Song of Simeon, St. Luke ii. 29. As an alternative, Psalm lxvii., *Deus misereatur*.

The *Creed*. The saying or singing of the Creed is the conclusion of the Service of *praise*. It is the response of the congregation to the readings from God's Revelation: 'Yes; we believe the glorious news.' So the Creed follows the Epistle and Gospel in the Communion Service.

[Creed—'*credo*,' the first word, as with 'Pater noster,' etc. Three forms of Creed are found in the Prayer Book.
1. As here, the '*Apostles*'.' The name was not meant to contrast it with other 'Creeds,' but to claim it as a summary of 'the Apostles' doctrine' (Acts ii. 42). It was a creed that took shape in

the Western (Latin) Church, and was used at first in Baptism and in the instruction belonging to it, and eventually in the Daily Services, which were of Western origin. In the Prayer Book it is used in the Daily Services, in Holy Baptism (and therefore in the Catechism), and in the Visitation of the Sick.

2. The '*Nicene.*' So called from the Council of Nicæa, the first General Council of the Church, held in A.D. 325. The Creed, however, adopted at that Council ended with the words, 'I believe in the Holy Ghost.' The longer form was first recognised at the fourth General Council, at Chalcedon, in 451. It is therefore a creed, in origin, of the Greek or Eastern Church (*see* note on p. 62).

3. The 'Confession of our Christian faith, commonly called the Creed of *St. Athanasius.*' This, as the title given to it in the Prayer Book implies, is not properly a 'Creed,' for it does not begin with 'I believe,' but a declaration or explanation of the doctrine of the Creed. 'Athanasian' can only mean that it embodies the belief for which Athanasius, the great opponent of Arius at the Council of Nicæa, contended. It is of much later origin than the Apostles' and Nicene Creed, and was written in Latin. It is therefore headed in the Prayer Book, with its first words, 'Quicunque Vult.' It has reference throughout to early heresies which its definitions are meant to meet point by point. It is ordered to be used in the place of the Apostles' Creed on certain days, viz. on chief Festivals, Christmas, The

Epiphany, Easter, The Ascension, Whitsunday, Trinity Sunday, and on other Holy Days, chosen apparently with a view to its being used about once a month.]

Then we pass to *Prayer.* (*See* the *Rubric.*)
  It is introduced by
> (1) the mutual salutation of Minister and people in scriptural words.
>> *M.* 'The Lord be with you.' (Ruth ii. 4. 2 Thess. iii. 16.)
>> *A.* 'And with thy spirit.' (2 Tim. iv. 22.)
> (2) the invitation to prayer.
> (3) the so-called 'Lesser Litany' (*see* p. 39), or cry for mercy to the Three Persons of the Blessed Trinity.

Then *The Lord's Prayer* (*see* p. 27), here without the doxology.

The *Versicles* which follow are taken generally (all but 'Give peace in our time') from the Psalms. Ps. lxxxv. 7; xx. 9; cxxxii. 9; li. 10, 11.

They put in a few words the objects for which we pray more fully afterwards, viz. intercession for the sovereign, for the clergy and people, prayers for peace (Second Collect) and grace (Third Collect).

The *Collect for the Day.* (*See* VII., p. 49.)
  The Collects in the Morning for *peace* and *grace*, in the Evening for *peace* and '*against all perils.*'
  Here again there is a break—the service until 1662 having ended at this point.

Anthem—More properly as in old writing 'antim.' It is a corruption of Antiphon, and was used properly of something sung 'antiphonally' by the two sides of the choir.

The remaining prayers were added in 1662, the *Prayer of St. Chrysostom* (so called — it is of early date, but not certainly traced to him) and the *Benediction*, from 2 Cor. xiii. 14, having been originally placed only at the end of the Litany.

[Note, in the prayer for clergy and people, the old phrase 'curates,' used not in our modern sense of 'deputies' or 'assistant clergy,' but as the Fr. *curé*, of persons *in charge* of souls.]

VI

THE LITANY

MEANING OF THE TERM, AND GENERAL HISTORY

NOTICE the alternative title, 'or *general supplication*.'

Litania—λιτανεία, subst. of λιτανεύω, verb frequent in Homer, in sense of 'to entreat,' 'to supplicate'—*earnest prayer*.

The term was particularly applied to prayers said by priests and people walking in procession, such prayers having the especial purpose of deprecating God's judgments in times of trouble and danger. There was a 'refrain' or answer chanted by the people, a very common one being Κύριε ἐλέησον (in Latin letters, 'Kyrie eleison'), 'Lord, have mercy on us.' From this the invocation of the Three Persons of the Holy Trinity: 'Lord, have mercy on us! Christ, have mercy on us! Lord, have mercy on us!' is often called the '*Lesser Litany*.'

The word for such 'Litanies' in the Western Church was '*Rogationes*,' from which our 'Rogation Days' get their name (*see* p. 11).

'Litanies' then were originally
(1) not services meant to be said in churches but to be sung in *processions*.
(2) *occasional*—not regular services, but extemporised in times of special danger or trouble. This is illustrated in the case of the earliest Western Litanies that we hear of. Thus
  (1) Mamertus, Bishop of Vienne (on the Rhone), instituted the Rogation Days, which afterwards became general, on the occasion of a succession of earthquakes in A.D. 467.
  (2) Gregory the Great (the Pope who sent Augustine to England) instituted a Litany at Rome in A.D. 590 on the occasion of a pestilence.—[we may remember the story of an angel being seen during the chanting of this Litany sheathing his sword over the Mausoleum of Hadrian, called thenceforth the Castle of St. Angelo.]

OUR OWN LITANY—ITS HISTORY

The Litany, which is based upon older forms, was the earliest service of our Prayer Book to be published in English. It was published alone in 1544, with a letter from Henry VIII. to Abp. Cranmer commending it to general use. This letter contains reminders of both the points noticed as to the original use of litanies — (1) it uses the word 'processions' as synonymous with 'litanies'—'processions said or sung'—though the service was by this time used in churches not in processions—(2) it gives as a reason for popularizing such a service the great troubles of the time, 'the miserable state of Christendom, being at this present time, besides other troubles, so plagued with the most cruel wars and dissensions.' Many phrases in the Litany bear the colour of that time or of times still remembered then—'from sedition, privy conspiracy,' 'from all false doctrine, heresy,' 'from battle and murder, and from sudden death,' 'all prisoners and captives,' 'our enemies, persecutors.' One famous 'deprecation' stood in the Litany as published under Henry VIII. and in the two Prayer Books of Edward VI., but was struck out of Elizabeth's; viz. after 'privy conspiracy,' 'from the tyranny of the Bishop of Rome and all his detestable enormities.' On the other hand, in the Prayer Book of 1662 after the Restoration in State and Church, two additions were made: (1) '*Rebellion*' after 'privy conspiracy,' (2) '*schism*' after 'heresy.'

THE CONTENTS

It may be divided into two parts.

I. The *Litany proper* which begins and ends with the Kyrie. This consists again of two parts.
 1. *Penitential and deprecatory*—consisting of
    (a) an expansion of the 'Lesser Litany' (*see* above), an address to each of the Three Persons of the Godhead and to the Undivided Trinity, confessing sin and praying for mercy.
    (b) what are usually called 'the Deprecations' —asking for deliverance from evil: spiritual, mental, moral, bodily.

[*N.B.*—That after the invocation of the Holy Trinity the prayers are all addressed to our Blessed Lord. This is clear from the words: 'whom Thou hast redeemed with Thy most precious Blood,' 'by Thy Cross and Passion,' etc. This continues till the repetition of the invocation in the 'Kyrie,' 'Lord, have mercy upon us,' etc., before the Lord's Prayer. The remaining prayers are addressed, as prayer more usually is, to God the Father through the intercession of God the Son.]

(*c*) what are sometimes called 'the Obsecrations' (a word that means 'specially earnest entreaties'), 'By the mystery of Thy Holy Incarnation,' etc. 'In all time of our tribulation,' etc. Some doubt has been felt as to the meaning of 'by' in these prayers. It may be taken (perhaps most naturally) of the *ground* of entreaty 'by all that Thou hast done and borne to help us before, help us now.' It has also been taken as meaning '*by virtue of* — make Thine Incarnation, Sufferings, Death, effectual to our deliverance.' The last place is, in any case, given to our own extreme need. After saying 'in time of our tribulation' we are taught to remember, in God's sight, that the time of 'wealth' (prosperity) is a time when we need God's deliverance even more, for it is a time of greater danger to us.

2. *Intercessory*—asking for blessings on others and on ourselves—on the Queen and all in authority—for the peace of the world—for virtue and religion at home—for the erring—the weak—for all in need—for all mankind—for our enemies—for blessings temporal and spiritual.

This part ends as the first began with the cry for mercy—'O Lamb of God,' etc. 'O Christ, hear us,' and the 'Kyrie.'

II. *Prayers and Versicles.*

This part begins, as prayer usually begins, with the Lord's Prayer (*see* p. 27). This is the reason why the Lord's Prayer comes in this particular place in the Litany.

NOTES ON WORDS AND PHRASES

FIRST PART.

O God the Father, of heaven. Notice the comma. 'Of heaven' is a translation of *de caelis*, and that of ἐξ οὐρανοῦ, St. Luke xi. 13; so that it is equivalent to 'which art in heaven' in the Lord's Prayer.

mischief—harm, calamity. (Originally 'bad result,' 'chief' is, through French *chef*, from Latin *caput* in the sense of 'ending,' 'completion,' cp. 'to achieve.')

crafts and assaults—whether he tries to beguile and deceive, or to surprise and force us.

damnation—condemnation.

hypocrisy—from Gr. ὑποκριτής, an actor—acting a part—insincerity.

world — flesh — devil — remember the Baptismal promise, and *cp.* Collect for Eighteenth Sunday after Trinity.

from all sedition, etc.—the sins prayed against in this petition are those of self-will, leading to the resistance of lawful authority, in the State, in the Church, in the personal relation of the soul to God and to conscience which is His Voice. Under each head each act named is an advance upon the last: Thus

(*a*) *sedition*—the spirit of faction and disloyalty.
privy conspiracy—plotting with others secretly.
rebellion—open or armed resistance.

(*b*) *false doctrine* — wrong teaching on religious matters.
heresy—the holding of doctrines actually condemned by the Church ($αἵρεσις$).
schism—wrong opinions carried to the point of positive separation ($σχίσμα$) from the body of the Church.

(*c*) So also hardness of heart, contempt of God's Word, and contempt of His commandment—a lawless *life* following on lawless *thought*.
mystery—used of truth believed because it is revealed, but wonderful to reason. It properly means 'a secret revealed.'
Incarnation—'The Word made Flesh.' St. John i. 14.
tribulation—crushing sorrow. It is used in the New Testament as a translation of $θλίψις$ (as Acts xiv. 22). *Tribulatio* is not a classical Latin

word, but is derived from *tribulum* (Virg. *Georg.* 1, 146), the heavy threshing sledge used instead of a flail to separate the husk from the corn.

wealth—not, as now, narrowed to 'riches,' but weal —happiness—prosperity.

Church universal—the same as the 'Church Catholic'—'the whole congregation of Christian people dispersed throughout the world.'

affiance — trust — loyalty, French *fier*, Old French also *afier*, Late Latin *adfidere*, *adfidare* (*cp.* our 'affidavit').

set it forth—*i.e.* by preaching truly. *Show it accordingly* (=correspondingly) by living in accordance with it.

endue—clothe—Lat. *induere*. *Cp.* Ps. cxxxii. 9.

Lords of the Council—this means, in effect, 'for the Queen's Ministers.' The Cabinet, or ruling Committee of Ministers, is in theory and historically a Committee of the Privy Council, chosen from the Party which is in the majority in Parliament at the time, for the confidential advice of the Sovereign. This distinction of the Cabinet from the larger Privy Council is of later date than the Prayer Book.

keep—protect, guide. Gen. xxviii. 15; 1 Sam. ii. 9, etc.

magistrates—judges—those who interpret and enforce the law.

to maintain truth.—This is one of the phrases which, in their proper sense, belong to the time when the Prayer Book was composed rather than to our own day. It meant 'to uphold true doctrines.' It was then thought by all parties alike that it was the duty of the State to repress religious error by civil penalties, even, if necessary, by the penalty of death. We have learnt that all such interference of the State in matters of opinion does harm instead of good to the truth.

love and dread—cp. Collect for Second Sunday after Trinity, 'a perpetual fear and love of Thy Holy Name.'

after—'secundum,' in accordance with. So in the versicles (*see* p. 28) after the Lord's Prayer, 'after our sins.'

meekly—St. James i. 21.

fruits of the Spirit—Gal. v. 22. The three stages of hearing, receiving, bringing forth the fruit, remind us of the Parable of the Sower.

erred—the preceding 'way of truth' reminds us that to 'err' (*errare*) is to wander.

beat down Satan.—Rom. xvi. 20.

all that travel.—There are special dangers still in travels both by land and sea, but they were very much greater then and even two centuries ago. (*See* Macaulay's *History*, ch. iii.)

prisoners and captives.—Particular occasions will give this petition peculiar force even in our own days, as in the Indian Mutiny or during the siege of Khartoum; but, as describing a class of persons to be always had in mind, it belonged more thoroughly to times of Christian captives in the hands of Algerine pirates, Englishmen in the hands of Spanish inquisitors, etc.

kindly fruits—'kindly' meant properly 'natural' —suitable to their kind or nature; so here, fruits at their proper season and in their natural quality and measure.

true repentance, etc.—Notice the order: (1) power to repent, (2) forgiveness, (3) power to amend. All are treated as coming from God and to be sought from Him. *Sins, negligences, ignorances*—three grades of offence, acts of conscious wrong, acts of thoughtless wrong, wrong acts which have proceeded from ignorance (1 Tim. i. 13).

O Lamb of God, etc.—St. John i. 29.

SECOND PART.

The Lord's Prayer—(*see* what was said on p. 27).

after our sins—(*see* above, p. 46). 'Use every man *after his deserts*, and which of us shall escape whipping?'—*Hamlet*, Act II., Sc. ii.

contrite—crushed—one that has had the crust of pride, evil habit, etc., broken. Ps. li. 17; Isaiah lvii. 15.

O God, we have heard, etc.—Ps. xliv. 1. Notice how, in this second part of the Litany, as in the end of so many Psalms of penitential supplication (such as Ps. xxii., lxix., lxxvii.), the key changes to greater 'quietness and confidence.'

It is worth noticing

(1) That the Prayer 'of St. Chrysostom' and the 'Grace of our Lord' in the earlier editions of the Prayer Book stood at the end of the Litany only, Morning and Evening Prayer ending with the Third Collect.

(2) That the 'occasional Prayers and Thanksgiving' which follow the Litany in the Prayer Book, and are ordered to be said 'before the two final Prayers of the Litany or Morning and Evening Prayer,' grew out of prayers for times of bad weather, famine, war, and plague or sickness, which, in the second Prayer Book of Edward VI., stood in the Litany before the Prayer of St. Chrysostom, thus belonging to the character of the Litany, already pointed out, as originally an occasional service having reference to some moment of special trouble. In 1662 some other occasional prayers were added and some corresponding thanksgivings, and they were separated from the Litany and ordered to be used as at present.

VII

COLLECTS, EPISTLES, AND GOSPELS

THE Collects, Epistles, and Gospels immediately precede, and belong to, the Order for the administration of the Holy Communion—being, in fact, that part of the order which changes from Sunday to Sunday and Holy Day to Holy Day. As the Collect is ordered to be used also in the Morning and Evening Prayer (*see* pp. 5, 37), it forms a link between the Daily Services and the Holy Communion, and therefore the Collects, Epistles, and Gospels stand fitly between them.

COLLECTS

1. The *origin of the name 'Collect'* has been a matter of dispute. *Collecta* is a late Latin word for 'a gathering' or assembly (it is so used in the Vulgate, *see* Lev. xxiii. 36), and, like the Greek σύναξις, which has the same meaning, it was used (1) of the assembling of the Church for Holy Communion; (2) of the Holy Communion itself. The particular prayer which formed a characteristic part of the Communion Service was called, it would seem, first *oratio ad collectam* [a phrase which is found], and then, more shortly, *collecta*

[Other more fanciful derivations have been suggested, as that it described a prayer which 'gathered,' summarized, the desires of the congregation, or which gathered the thoughts of the Epistle and Gospel.]

Source of our Collects.

Most of them are ancient, being found, appropriated as at present to particular Sundays and Holy Days, in the earliest Roman 'Sacramentaries' (books of sacramental services), viz. those which are attributed to the Popes Gelasius (end of fifth century) and Gregory the Great (end of sixth century). This would mean, no doubt, that many of the prayers themselves were older than the collections in which they appear. Some of our Collects, on the other hand, are of the date of our Book of Common Prayer—viz. of those included in it in 1549, the Collects for Second Sunday in Advent, Quinquagesima, First Sunday in Lent, Second Sunday after Easter, and a good many Holy Days; in 1552, for St. Andrew; and in 1662, for Third Sunday in Advent, Sixth Sunday after Epiphany, and Easter Eve. It will be seen that several of our most beautiful Collects are peculiar to our own Prayer Book.

Character of a Collect.

The Collects have always been admired as one of the most perfect features of the Church Prayers. They are marked by their devout and sober tone, their choice language and rhythm, their brevity, and the unity and completeness of the composition. None exceeds the limits of a sentence, generally a short one.

This comprehends—

(1) A devout address to Almighty God. Notice that where, as is very frequently the case, this recalls some special act or revealed attribute of God, these are most closely related to the petition which is to follow. In this the Collects follow the model of the Lord's Prayer, in which the petitions grow naturally out of the twofold address: 'Our Father, which art in heaven.'

(2) A petition, often accompanied by a clause expressing the special purpose or expected result of the petition.

(3) Either (as in most cases) a mention of our Lord's merits as the ground of appeal—'through Jesus Christ our Lord,' or similar words—or an ascription of praise (as on Trinity Sunday). Sometimes, especially on the great Festivals, we find both (as on Christmas Day).

Connection of the Collects with the Epistles and Gospels.

Some correspondence between them seems to be supposed, but it varies in kind and in closeness according to circumstances. It is most evident on the great Festivals and on Holy Days generally, when Collect, Epistle, and Gospel all turn on the special subject of the day. The same is the case in the seasons of Advent and Lent, when the subject each week is some aspect of Christ's Coming or of Repentance and Forgiveness. On the Sundays after Easter there are two clues to the subjects of the Collects as of the

Epistles and Gospels. On the one hand, they belong to the period between the Resurrection and Ascension (Collect for First Sunday, and the Gospels generally). On the other they bear reference (the remaining Collects and the Epistles generally) to the fact that Easter was the chief time for Baptism, and are therefore prayers and readings for the newly baptized.

THE EPISTLES AND GOSPELS

The Epistles and Gospels are a part of our Service taken directly from the ancient Service Book of the English Church. The selection is substantially that of a Table called *Comes* ('the companion' or 'vademecum'), which bears the name of St. Jerome (who died A.D. 420), and which, though its connection with him is uncertain, is of great antiquity. As the Holy Communion was the Sunday Service of the ancient Church the Epistles and Gospels were its Sunday Lessons.

The principle of selection seems to be different for the two halves of the Church year. From Advent to Trinity Sunday both the Epistles and Gospels are chosen to illustrate the teaching of the special season, the Gospels giving, if read together, a consecutive narrative of the chief events in the Gospel history. On the remaining Sundays the Epistles seem to have been the first selected, as these follow, to a great extent, the principle of consecutive reading from each of the chief Epistles in order (a principle of which there have been some signs before, in the readings from Romans xii. and xiii. on the Sundays after

Epiphany, and from St. Peter and St. James on the Sundays after Easter), the Gospels being chosen as enforcing partially or wholly the same lesson as the Epistles.

The 'Epistle' is taken twelve times from the Acts, on Holy Days where the narrative required could be found there better than in the Gospels. It is taken four times (on Trinity Sunday and on three Holy Days) from the Revelation; and seven times (on the twenty-fifth Sunday after Trinity and on six Holy Days) from the Prophets of the Old Testament.

VIII

THE ORDER OF THE ADMINISTRATION OF THE LORD'S SUPPER OR HOLY COMMUNION

NOTES ON THE TITLE

1. *Order.*—The usual name in the Prayer Book for the fixed form of some service. So 'Order for Morning Prayer,' 'Order of Confirmation.' It is a similar expression to the Latin title 'Canon Missae' (κανών, 'rule'), though that is applied only to the central part of the Service.

2. *Administration.*—So, in the first exhortation after the Prayer for the Church militant, 'I purpose ... to *administer* to all such as shall be religiously disposed, etc.' Similarly the Baptismal Services are headed, 'the Ministration of Publick Baptism of infants,' 'the Ministration of Baptism to such as are of riper years.'

It expresses the offering of the Sacrament to individuals through the agency of God's ministers.

Another phrase (used in several rubrics, and in the first sentence of the second exhortation) is '*celebration*,' 'to celebrate the Lord's "Supper."' This is from the Latin verb *celebrare* (*convivium, nuptias, sacra*), to 'solemnize publicly, in the presence of a gathering of people.'

3. *Lord's Supper.*—The phrase comes from 1 Cor. xi. 20: κυριακὸν δεῖπνον, *dominica cena*, 'the Lord's,' because instituted by Him, because He is the Host, and we the guests. 'Supper,' because it always carries the remembrance of the Holy Supper at which it was instituted (1 Cor. xi. 25). In the same way the Prayer Book always uses the title, 'The Table,' 'The Lord's Table' (in the earlier edition, 'God's Board).' For this title, *see* 1 Cor. x. 21.

4. *Holy Communion.* From 1 Cor. x. 16, κοινωνία, *communio*, the act of partaking or fellowship. St. Paul there explains the word as implying that it is an act of close fellowship both with Christ and with our brethren. From this name come the words 'communicate' and 'communicant.'

5. Another name frequently given, although not used in the Prayer Book, is *Eucharist*—εὐχαριστία, 'an act of thanksgiving.' It is derived from the verb constantly used of our Lord's acts in instituting it: 'He blessed,' 'He gave thanks' (εὐλογεῖν, εὐχαριστεῖν, the two verbs being identical in meaning in this use), St. Matt. xxvi. 27. In 1 Cor. xiv. 16, the substantive εὐχαριστία, 'giving of thanks,' seems to be used for the utterance of the Minister in celebrating the Lord's Supper.

6. Two other words may be here explained:
    (1) *Liturgy*, used often in English of the whole Prayer Book (as in the first Preface), but in ancient times it was more usual to restrict its meaning to the office of Holy Communion.

Λειτουργία meant properly 'public service,' its classical use being of the services to the State which at Athens were provided, not by general taxation, but by assignment in rotation to the richer citizens. In the LXX. it was used for the 'public service' of God in the Temple, and in ecclesiastical Greek it became the name of the distinctive services of Christian assemblies.

(2) *Missa*, the Latin name; French *messe*; English *mass*. The word was retained in the first Prayer Book (1549), 'The Supper of the Lorde and the Holy Communion, commonly called the Masse.' After that it was dropped out of use, but remains in the words Christ-mas, Michael-mas, etc. The word seems to have had no signification in itself, being taken from the phrase with which the Latin service ended, 'Ite, missa est,' where *missa* probably corresponded to *collecta* (*see* p. 49), and meant the 'dismissal' of the congregation. The book that contained the service was called 'Missale,' a Missal, or, in older Latin (*see* p. 50), 'Sacramentarium.'

NOTE ON THE LAST RUBRIC BEFORE THE SERVICE

It is to be noticed that the attitude of the Priest in Prayer throughout the Communion Service (except in the Confession and the Prayer, 'we do not presume etc.,' in which especial humility is expressed) is *standing*. This is one illustration of the antiquity of the service.

Two attitudes of prayer are seen in the Bible to have been recognised among the Jews:

(1) *standing*—1 Sam. i. 26; St. Matt. vi. 5; St. Luke xviii. 11.
(2) *kneeling*—1 Kings viii. 54; Dan. vi. 10.

Both were adopted into the Christian Church, but there was a special rule that prayer always on the Lord's Day, and in the period between Easter and Whitsunday, should be offered *standing*. We have a survival of this in the attitude of the Priest in the Communion and in the Versicles in the Daily Services. In the Scottish Presbyterian Church standing was till lately the attitude of prayer in the whole congregation. In our usage kneeling has, except in this instance, become the normal attitude.

HISTORY

The Communion Service is, in substance, the oldest part of the Prayer Book, though, like other services, it was rearranged in the order of its several parts.

It appears in the New Testament that the Lord's Supper formed from the first the central act of the weekly meeting of Christians on the Lord's Day (*see*, amongst other places, Acts xx. 7, where, as in Acts ii. 42, 46, it is called 'breaking of bread;' *cp.* also 1 Cor. x. 16); but the only notice of any form of service is in 1 Cor. xiv. 16, where we hear of a thanksgiving uttered by some one in authority and responded to with 'Amen' from the congregation. From 1 Cor. xi. we learn that the association of the Lord's Supper with the common meal, although in accordance with the precedent of its institution at the Last Supper, had led to grave scandals, and the two seem to have been separated.

A short account, evidently from hearsay, and with imperfect understanding of what he reported, is given in the letter in which Pliny describes (*Epp.* x. 97, about A.D. 103) to the Emperor Trajan the practices of the Christians whom he found in his province (Bithynia): 'They affirmed,' he says, 'that the sum-total of their fault, if you will, or their delusion, was that they were wont, on an appointed day, to meet before it was light, and sing one to another a hymn addressed to Christ as a god, and bind themselves by an oath ('sacramento'), not to any wickedness, but not to commit theft, robbery, adultery, not to break their word or refuse to restore a pledge; that after this their custom was to separate, and meet again later in the day to eat together, but only a public and innocent meal.'

About fifty years later (A.D. 150) we have in Justin Martyr's *Apology*, or defence of Christianity, addressed to the Emperor Antoninus Pius, a description, from inside, of a Christian meeting: 'On the day of the sun, as it is called, we all meet, whether we live in town or in the country, and the memoirs ($ἀπομνημο$-$νεύματα$) of the Apostles or the writings of the Prophets are read as time allows. Then, when the reader has finished, the president ($ὁ\ πρόεδρος$) essays to admonish and exhort us to put in practice the good things we have heard. Then we all rise and pray, and when we have finished prayer, as I said before, bread is brought, and wine and water, and the president offers up prayers at once and thanksgiving to the utmost of his power,[1] and the people shout an approving "Amen," and then those things for which thanks have been given are distributed to and shared by all who are present, and a portion is sent to those who are absent by the deacons.' We have here the elements of our own service: the reading of Scripture, the sermon, prayer, the consecration, and reception. Justin also mentions (1) an offertory for the benefit of those in need, (2) the kiss of peace, which formed part of all early liturgies.

Gradually, no doubt, and with varieties in one Church and another, the Scripture to be read and the prayers to be said became fixed. Many such 'Liturgies' are extant, some of them going by the name of Apostles, as of St. James, St. Mark, etc., and belonging to different ancient Churches, Palestine, Egypt, etc., but their date is uncertain. In the Western Church the variations in different dioceses, or groups of dioceses, were called *usus*, as the Gallican use, the Ambrosian use (at Milan), the use of Sarum, etc.

At the time of the Reformation, though the celebration of 'Mass' was the chief church service, reception of the Communion by the laity had become infrequent—the aspect of the service as one of Communion was lost sight of. The desire of our Reformers was to bring this aspect forward prominently, and

---

[1] ὅση δύναμις αὐτῷ. The words occur in another place, chap. xiii., ὅση δύναμις αἰνοῦντες [τὸν Δημιουργὸν τοῦδε τοῦ πάντος], 'praising the Creator to the utmost of our power.' The words express the fervour of the prayer and thanksgiving. They suggest, though they do not necessarily imply, extempore prayer.

their changes in the service were directed to fit it for this end.

N.B.—In the *Rubrics* at the end of the Service the Priest is forbidden to celebrate the Lord's Supper unless there be a definite number to communicate with him.

DIVISIONS OF THE SERVICE

The Service begins with the Lord's Prayer (always the beginning of prayers, *see* p. 27) and the prayer for purity of heart, to worship aright. It then divides itself into three parts:

1. The Ante-Communion, or service of preparation.
2. The Consecration and Communion.
3. The Post-Communion, or service of thanksgiving.

I. THE ANTE-COMMUNION.

This again is twofold. The first part, which ends with the 'Prayer for the whole state of Christ's Church militant here on earth,' may be used when there is no Communion. (*See* Rubric 1 at the end of the Service.)

It is after this that we find the exhortations placed, both for giving notice of a celebration of the Holy Communion, and to the communicants at the time.

The two parts represent two stages in preparation, the first preparatory to the second. The idea of both is expressed by the Church in the last question and

THE COMMUNION SERVICE

answer of the Catechism, in which we are told that the requisites for right coming to the Lord's Supper are:

(1) Repentance, including a steadfast purpose of amendment.
(2) Faith, including a thankful remembrance of Christ's Death.
(3) Charity towards all men.

The readings from Holy Scripture and the Sermon are intended to move us to all or some of these.

> To (1) belong, in the *first* part of the Ante-Communion,
>> The Commandments, with the petition in each case, 'Incline our hearts,' etc.
>> [The reading of the Ten Commandments in the Ante-Communion was a novelty in the English Prayer Book. It is found first in the Prayer Book of 1552. The purpose was to guide people in *self-examination* at a time when private confession to the priest was no longer required, as it had been in Roman usage, as a condition of Communion. It will be remembered that the keeping of the Ten Commandments was one of the promises in Baptism and Confirmation.]
>> In the *second*, and more personal part, the Confession.

To (2) belong, in the *first* part, the Creed.¹
    in the *second*, the Absolution and the 'Comfortable Words;'
    the 'Ter Sanctus,' 'Holy, Holy, Holy,' and its Prefaces (the faith of praise, joy);
    the 'Prayer of humble access,' 'We do not presume,' etc. (the faith of humble trust, recalling the faith of the Syro-Phœnician woman, St. Mark vii. 28.)

To (3) belong (1) the offertory, *giving*, as a result of charity. (*See* the command in Deut. xvi. 16.)
    (2) the prayer 'for the whole state of Christ's Church militant here on earth,' for the Church fighting against evil on earth, opposed to the Church at rest, or triumphant, in another life. Prayer for all implies caring for all.

II. THE CONSECRATION AND COMMUNION.

The Prayer of Consecration.

1. Note that it is called a 'Prayer,' and that the people say 'Amen' to it. The Priest is representing the congregation even here. *Cp.* the account given by Justin Martyr (p. 58) of the primitive practice.

---

¹ See p. 36. That the 'Nicene' rather than the 'Apostles'' Creed is used in the office of Holy Communion in the whole Western Church is due to the fact that the Service was the earliest to be put into formal shape, and that before the Eastern and Western Churches were divided.

2. The narrative of the Institution, 'Who in the same night,' and what follows, is so given as to weave together our Lord's words from the four accounts, St. Matt. xxvi., St. Mark xiv., St. Luke xxii., 1 Cor. xi.

The Communion.

The words of administration consist in each case of two clauses. In King Edward VI.'s First Book, the first clause only was used. In King Edward VI.'s Second Book this was dropped and the second clause substituted for it.

In Queen Elizabeth's revision the two were put together as they are now. Notice that the two together correspond to the two clauses in our Lord's words of institution: 'This is My Body,' 'Do this in remembrance of Me.'

III. THE POST-COMMUNION.

The *Lord's Prayer.* Notice (1) its repetition here, where prayer is beginning again; (2) that occurring in a service of thanksgiving it has the doxology. (*See* p. 27.)

The *prayer of sacrifice.* In virtue of the great sacrifice which has just been commemorated we venture to offer

(1) the 'sacrifice of praise and thanksgiving' (*See* Heb. xiii. 15);
(2) 'ourselves, our souls, and bodies' (*See* Rom. xii. 1);

or the alternative prayer of *thanksgiving.*

www.ingramcontent.com/pod-product-compliance
Lightning Source LLC
Chambersburg PA
CBHW020253090426
42735CB00010B/1903